DATE DUE			

HIGHSMITH #45114

Nature Upclose

A Luna Moth's Life

Written and Illustrated by John Himmelman

Children's Press®
A Division of Grolier Publishing
New York London Hong Kong Sydney
Danbury, Connecticut

For Gary and Carol Lemmon
May our paths continue to cross
as we watch, listen, learn,
and spread the word.

Library of Congress Cataloging-in-Publication Data

Himmelman, John
    A luna moth's life / written and illustrated by John Himmelman
       p.   cm. — (Nature upclose)
    Summary: Illustrations and simple text describe the life cycle
of a luna moth.
    ISBN 0-516-20821-7
    1. Luna moth—Juvenile literature. 2. Luna moth —
Life cycles — Juvenile literature.   [1. Luna moth 2. Moth]
I. Title. II. Series:
    Himmelman, John.   Nature upclose.
    QL561.s2H55   1998
    595.78—dc21   97-20016
                                        CIP
                                        AC

Visit Children's Press on the Internet at:
http://publishing.grolier.com

Luna Moth
Actias luna

The luna moth is common in forested areas throughout the eastern United States and southeastern Canada. In the north, the caterpillars eat the leaves of white birch trees. In the south, they feed on walnut and hickory leaves.

The adult luna moth comes out of its cocoon in the late spring or early summer in the north. In the south, the moth can come out at any time of year. As a result, up to three generations of lunas can live in one year. Adults die within a week of mating. They do not have working mouthparts, so they cannot eat or drink.

The name "luna" means "moon" in Latin. The moth was named after the moon because it is active only at night. The luna caterpillar and pupa are active during the day.

Luna moths are often attracted to bright lights. Be sure to look for them around outdoor lights on summer evenings.

One night in late spring, a luna moth lays her eggs on a leaf.

A week later, the luna *larvae*—or caterpillars—begin to hatch.

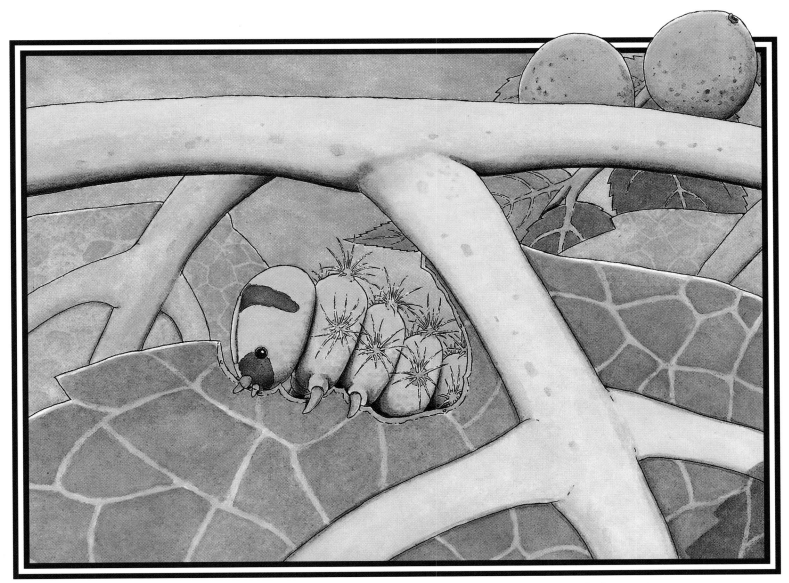

Each caterpillar goes off on its own in search of food.

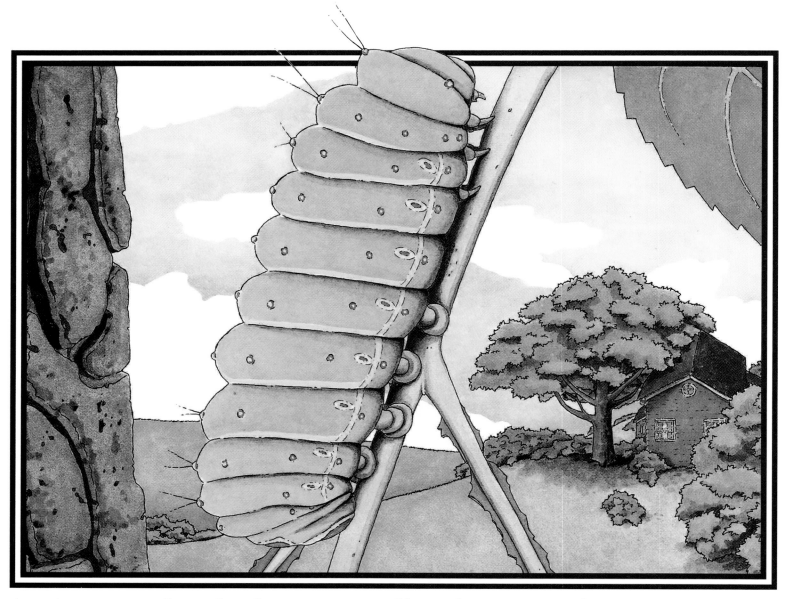

As time goes by, the luna caterpillar changes and grows.

Luckily, a hunting hornet does not see her!

In early summer, the luna larva begins to change.

The luna wraps herself in a leaf and glues it closed with silk.

Autumn leaves cover the *cocoon*. It is hard to find,
even for a *flicker*.

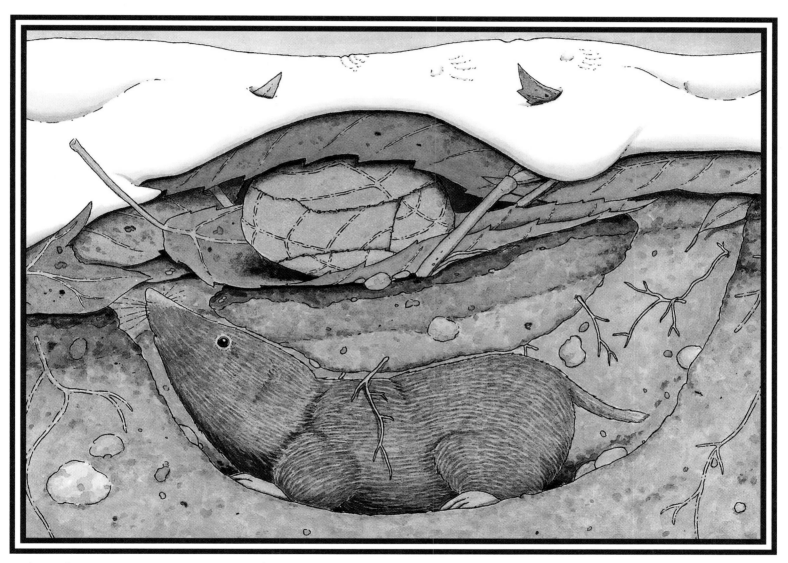

The luna *pupa* spends winter wrapped in her cocoon.

On a late spring morning, the cocoon begins to move.

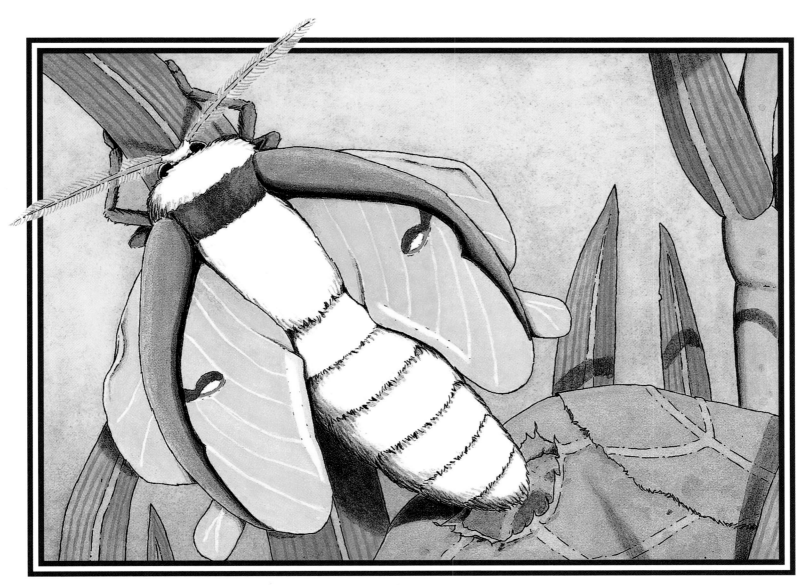

Out crawls the adult luna moth.

She climbs up a branch to dry out her wings.

Her wings slowly unfold in the breeze.

By evening, the luna moth is ready to fly.

A bright light attracts her.

She flies through an open window.

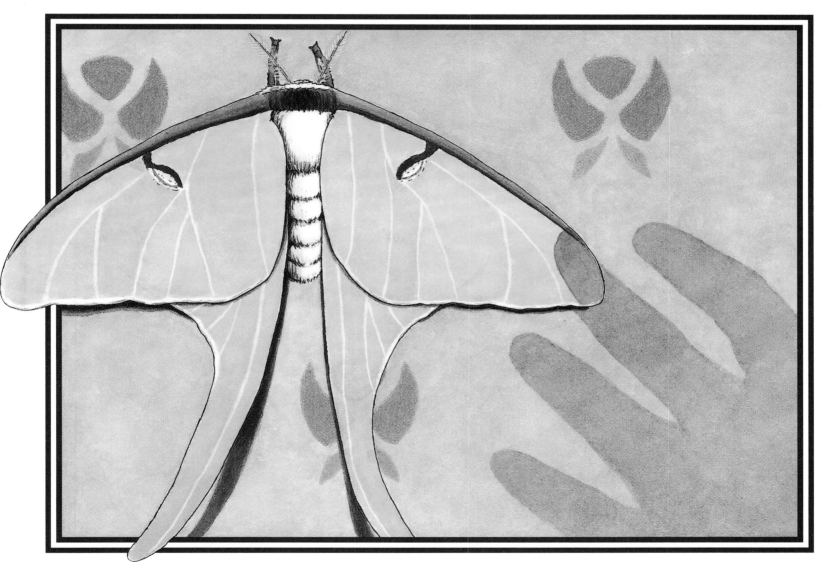

She rests on a wall.

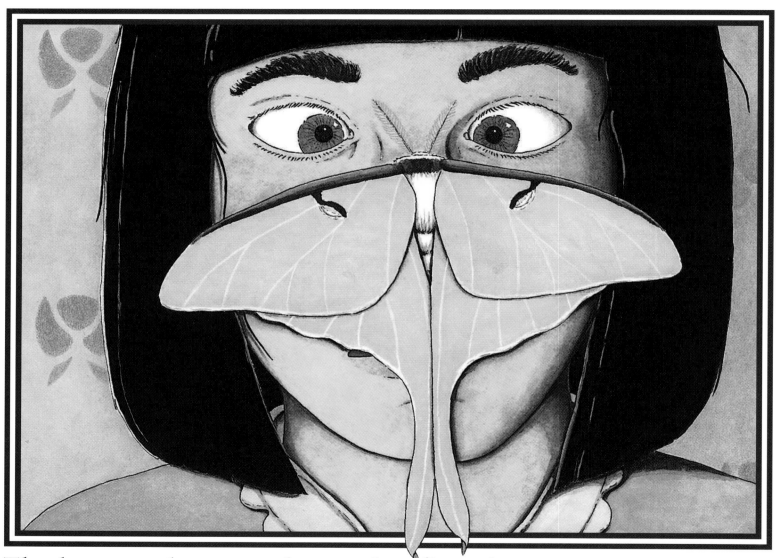

The luna moth senses danger, but flies the wrong way.

But there is no real danger. A child sets her free.

The luna moth cruises through the night sky.

She lands on a tree and sends out a silent call.

A male picks up her signal with his feathery *antennae*.

After they mate, the luna lays her eggs under the midnight moon.

Then she hides among the leaves until the next night.

But a gust of wind blows her from the tree.

A *bluejay* snaps at her, but only gets a piece of wing.

The luna moth has plenty of wing to spare.

When night returns, she flies and flies under the moon.

Words You Know

antennae (sing. antenna)—the pair of slender sensory organs on the heads of insects and some other animals.

bluejay—a blue, white, and gray bird that is common throughout North America. Its call sounds like the word "jay."

cocoon—a covering that a pupa builds around itself while it transforms into an adult insect.

flicker—a large woodpecker that is common throughout North America.

larvae (sing. larva)—the first stage of an insect's life.

pupa—the second stage of an insect's life.

About the Author

John Himmelman has written or illustrated more than forty books for children, including *Ibis: A True Whale Story, Wanted: Perfect Parents,* and *J.J. Versus the Babysitter.* His books have received honors such as Pick of the List, Book of the Month, JLG Selection, and the ABC Award. He is also a naturalist who enjoys turning over dead logs, crawling through grass, kneeling over puddles, and gazing at the sky. His greatest joy is sharing these experiences with others. John lives in Killingworth, Connecticut, with his wife Betsy who is an art teacher. They have two children, Jeff and Liz.